POTTY TRAINING PUPPIES & DOGS - THE SIMPLE LITTLE GUIDE

Quickly and Easily Housebreak Your Puppy or Grown up Fur Ball

THE WOOF BROTHERS

Paperback ISBN: 978-3-96772-079-2

Hardcover ISBN: 978-3-96772-080-8

Cover Design by Teofan Gavriliu.

The Icons used in this work were designed by:

- Freepik, pch.vector, Stories, macrovector, ntl-studio, classicvector, inspiring, atharuah_, Eucalyp

Published by Admore Publishing: Berlin, Germany

Printed in the United States of America

www.admorepublishing.com

Contents

Training

An Introduction to Potty Training

The relationship between dogs and humans goes back a long time. In fact, historians estimate that we have been living with our furry best friends for about 14,000 years. That is nearly three times longer than we have been writing anything in *any* language!

But, while it might have been relatively simple for our ancient ancestors to live in the wild with their dogs, things have gotten a lot more complicated. You might not have cared if your dog had a potty accident next to your campfire when you weren't going to be there the next day anyway, but when you are talking hardwood floors under your dinner table, things are a little different!

Bringing a new dog home is awesome. Whether it is a new puppy or an older dog you have adopted, there is nothing like the instant bond we feel with our canine companions of choice. Humans and dogs are made to be together. ... But, when you step in the umpteenth wet patch on the carpet or discover that your new roomie is a sneaky pooper who likes to do their business in tucked-away corners, it is hard to feel the warm fuzzies!

We have been living and working with dogs for a long time. We spent years working in boarding kennels, in grooming parlors, and with dog trainers. We know there are a few deal-breakers that owners just can't get past. Toilet trouble is pretty much at the top of everyone's list!

But before you assume you need to choose between your dog or a hygienic home, you should know that most potty-training problems have a definite cause and a definite solution. Whatever the age or stage of your dog, and whatever the reason for their potty issues, there are real steps you can take to help solve the problem. They are not complicated or expensive. But they will take a little faith in your good boy or girl's ability to change, and some patience and perseverance from you.

Where You Are Now

If you are like most people, when you brought your dog home the very first time, you had big dreams about games of tug of war, snuggles on the couch, and unconditional devotion. You got all of that, but you also got a few things you weren't prepared for.

Puddles on the rug. Marking their territory. Way too many smelly accidents for your liking.

The first few times, you chalked it up to the new surroundings, but now, even though you love your dog, you are wondering if you are ever going to be able to share your home with them.

The good news is that you can. Nearly every type of potty problem with dogs has a solution, and in this book, we will look at what they are. We are not just going to look at potty training your new puppy (*although that is in here too!*) We are also going to look at how to manage toilet troubles with older dogs.

We will look at all the common causes of this problem and identify red flags that might be a warning sign of something else.

What You Will Learn

Reading this book, you will learn some of the most common reasons why your dog might be urinating or defecating in your house. In addition, you will learn the best way to approach each scenario.

We will also go over the potential health red flags that you might want to address if you have had your dog a while and they have suddenly developed this problem.

Just like every fur ball is a unique individual, the reason they are having this problem may also be due to a unique reason. Still, you are sure to find something in here that helps address the problem. We aim to provide simple, actionable steps you can take to solve the problem.

Because this is a much broader topic than most people imagine, it is broken into sections and chapters. Each of these will look at some of the situations and factors that might be related to your doggo's problem. You may find that more than one of these applies to your situation. They include:

- A dog-friendly environment. What can you do to set your dog up for success!
- Dog training supplies. Yes, you are going to need some. We will tell you which ones!
- Common myths & misconceptions. There are lots of old wives' tales out there!
- Dog food and digestion. The food you are choosing might be contributing to potty problems!
- Training strategies that reinforce the positive rather than the negative.
- Creating a schedule for your dog.
- Solutions to common issues and potential puppy potty pitfalls.

The most important thing to remember is that there is nearly always a solution to the problem you are having. You don't have to choose between your dog and your home. You can have both.

In nearly fifteen years of working with dogs and many more owning them, we have never met a dog that could not be trained at all. Even when an older dog is resistant to new tricks, there are always strategies you can use.

You can share your home, your life, and your floors with your furry companion without conflict. So, take a deep breath, read on, and get ready to change how you live with your pup.

EVERYTHING I KNOW I LEARNED FROM DOGS.

- Nora Roberts

ONE

Ages and Stages

Most people assume that when you are looking for information about potty training your dog, you are talking about a puppy.

However, more people than ever are adopting older dogs, some of which may be set in their ways, have health conditions, or have other issues that you need to address. Therefore, before we get into specifics, we should look at how your dog's age and other factors might affect how you potty train.

Puppies

Believe it or not, puppies are the easiest dogs to train. It might not seem like it when they are singing the song of their people at 3am, or when you have another puddle to clean up. Still, because they don't have any habits formed yet, it is relatively straightforward to steer them towards behavior you want to become a habit.

When you are potty training a puppy, consistency and pre-emptive strategies work best. You want to take your puppy outside or to wherever their toilet area will be regularly before they even start sniffing around. They will soon get the idea, and the accidents will become few and far between.

As they start to become more of your family, as long as you consistently reinforce and reward the behavior you want, they'll definitely start doing things the way you prefer.

Never discipline a puppy for an accident, though! Negative reinforcement will only make it harder to get them to do things the way you want them done. Instead, hugs, snuggles, praise, and lots of love will do wonders!

Older Dogs New to Your Home

When you adopt an older dog that is new to your home, you also adopt all of their learned behaviors. This might be from their former home, or from a kennel, or similar.

When these 4 legged boys and girls are in a shelter or kennel, they don't really have the option of doing their "business" outside. So they might have become used to doing it, for instance, on a concrete floor. Which might be why you find puddles in the basement!

Sometimes, a previous owner will teach them bad habits too. For example, we once knew a Yorkshire Terrier who belonged to an elderly lady who trained him to go to the toilet on newspaper. So it was not really all that surprising that he treated every piece of paper that happened to be on the floor in his new home as a toilet!

Even though this can be frustrating for you, it is not actually their fault. But just like unwanted habits can be learned, they can be unlearned too.

Older dogs may benefit from having their living area limited for a few days, perhaps in a large crate or a dog run. Take them out frequently to the place you want them to go to the toilet, and whenever they ask to go out, make sure you are ready to take them!

If you adopt a dog used to using an indoor "pee pad," you might want to start with getting one of them and putting it in an easy-to-access spot. Then, gradually move it a little further towards where you want it until, eventually, it is outside their doggy door.

It can be harder to train older dogs than puppies, but it is entirely possible if you stick to it.

Territory Markers

Unfortunately, in older dogs (*particularly intact males*), potty accidents might not be accidents at all. Instead, they are territory marking behavior. This can be a problem when the territory being marked is your sofa or drapes!

Sometimes, dogs will suddenly start doing this when there is a significant life change – maybe you have moved, adopted a new animal, or had a baby. If so, this is almost certainly a psychological trigger. Therefore, while you are working on the problem, you need to pay your dog extra positive attention to reassure them that they are still loved and safe.

When dogs are marking territory rather than just going to the toilet, it can be harder to break the habit.

You will probably notice that this behavior happens in particular places and situations. For example, your dog may be smelling an old scent from another animal, which is why it is a good idea to thoroughly clean the areas that are a problem.

Keeping your dog out of the areas where they tend to do this is another good idea, as is, again, restricting them to a dog run or crate while training them not to do this.

There are commercial sprays on the market that can discourage marking, but very often, this problem is solved by ensuring that your dog goes out frequently. This way, there's "nothing in the tank."

Medical Related Incontinence

The final issue you need to be aware of is that sometimes, toilet trouble is involuntary.

This might be because your sweet pooch has gotten a bit older and lost muscle tone. Especially if they are female and have had puppies!

In other cases, particularly in younger dogs, sudden onset incontinence can signify something more serious. If your dog has never had this problem before and suddenly starts having accidents with no other apparent cause, you probably want to consult your veterinarian.

If your dog's accidents are related to age or a medical condition, no amount of training will solve the problem. You will need to address the underlying cause.

Doggy diapers can help older dogs that are experiencing age-related incontinence. However, medication or even surgery may be required to solve other medical-related problems.

Nervous Dogs

If your doggo is very excitable and highly strung, or they are very nervous, they may also pee without even realizing they are doing it.

If you have a little dog, that is probably not a huge problem. Still, we once had an eight-month-old Great Dane that was taller than us on his hind legs sprinkle one of us over our whole lower body with pee. This was all out of uncontrollable joy and excitement about the fact of seeing us. Still, it was quite the soggy issue!

If your 4 legged friend wets themselves when they are very happy or scared, you need to work on their behavioral issues if you want to solve the problem.

Not Just a Puppy Problem

As you can see, while we expect puddles from puppies, they are not the only ones that might have some toilet issues.

If you bring a new dog of any age home, you can expect a few bumps along the road, but patience and perseverance will solve the problem.

If your dog has a behavioral issue related to their toilet habits, you need to address the problem or keep them away from things that might trigger them. It is relatively easy to keep nervous or very excitable dogs away from situations that might cause the problem.

Finally, remember that if incontinence is a sudden onset issue, particularly in younger dogs, there may be a medical cause. Never ignore this! If your pup has never had this issue before, and it happens more than a handful of times in a short time span, you need to speak to your vet. It might be a normal side effect of aging, but it could be something more serious that requires medical treatment.

DOGS DO SPEAK, BUT ONLY TO THOSE WHO KNOW HOW TO LISTEN.

- Orhan Pamuk

TWO

Creating a Dog Friendly Environment

"Happiness is a warm puppy." – Charles Shultz

Charles Shultz created Snoopy, one of the most popular and well-loved dog characters in history. So, the man knew a thing or two about puppies.

But while there is no denying that puppies are happiness wrapped up in fur, they are also a **BIG** adjustment in a formerly dogless home.

Modern homes are made for human comfort. But they are not really ideally suited to our canine friends. So, if you are bringing your first puppy home and you want to set yourself up for success, you need to make a few changes.

Small things that we take for granted, like slippery floors and access to various parts of the home, are all part of creating a dog-friendly environment.

Smaller Spaces Work Better for Potty Training

When you are first potty training a puppy, you will need to spend a lot of time watching them for signs that they need to go to the bathroom. These might range from suddenly freezing in the middle of play and getting a vacant expression (particularly in younger puppies) to sniffing around for the perfect spot.

You might miss the first few signs, but you will soon learn what to look for.

Of course, puppies get into everything, so the smaller you can make the space you need to watch, the easier it will be to see when you need to make a dash outside or to their pee pad!

This works for older dogs that you have rehomed too. You don't know their habits yet, so it is easier to restrict their movements while establishing a routine.

Use portable dog runs, large crates, or even baby gates to section off smaller areas of your home where your new puppy or dog should stay while you're potty training them. Then watch them closely when they are outside of those areas!

If you do go with a dog run or crate, remember that this is NOT punishment. Instead, make this space warm and welcoming. Larger spots can even have a pillow to sleep on and their favorite toys.

Puppy and Dog Proofing

It is worth noting that while this book is mainly about potty training a puppy or dog, there are other types of puppy or dog proofing that you might want to think about while you keep them in a smaller area and establish a routine.

Make sure that you remove plants that might be chewed from places they can reach. Some plants can be toxic or even deadly if chewed, and even if they are not, you are not going to love it if your new pal turns your fern into a doggy salad!

The same goes for things like shoes. Yes. Puppies will chew them if they can. It is not their fault! Shoes are just so darn interesting, and once those little teeth come in, they have to do something, right?

Slippery floors are another puppy and pooch pitfall. If you have wooden floors that could be scratched and damaged, now is the time to invest in mats! Get the rubber-backed kind, so they won't slip all over the place.

Even if you are planning to take your new dog outside for bathroom breaks (or have a doggy door), it is a good idea to invest in some commercial pee pads that are absorbent. It is also a good idea to put them on a plastic tray (shoe trays work great) in case there are any leaks. Some owners decide to purchase faux grass pee pads. These are particularly useful for dogs that will be doing some of their potty breaks indoors as they grow up. It helps to prevent confusion between "going" outside on the lawn and inside your home.

Potty Training Supplies

Aside from the very basics that we have already covered, several items will make potty training your new 4 legged roommate a lot easier. There are various brands of all of these on the market, so you can try a few and choose whatever works for you.

A Doggy Door

If you will be letting your puppy or dog do their business outside on their own, it is a good idea to get a dog door and install it as soon as possible. Your pupper will quickly get used to the idea that they can let themselves out when they want to or need to. You can get these to fit most doors – there are even some that work with sliding doors, and many are lockable, so you can keep it closed for security reasons when you need to.

A Crate and Dog Run

Many people feel that crate training is punishment, but it is really not. As long as the crate is large enough and comfortable for your pup! A dog or puppy run with a floor protector of some kind will help while you are still in the "accident" phase. A crate is both a comfy bed to take a snooze in and an easy way to ensure that you don't have too many accidents.

This is particularly useful for older dogs that you might have adopted if you're not going to be home for a while. Most dogs will not "go" where they sleep, and if you are heading to the grocery store and take them out before and after, you can save your carpets and floors!

Pee Pads

We have already mentioned this, but I can't overstate the difference between newspaper and actual pee pads! These have a plastic backing, so they don't leak, and they have an absorbent layer, similar to what you find in diapers, on top. Therefore, they will not soak through like newspapers, and they are easy to clean up when there is an accident.

Some people who have small dogs choose to have a pee pad available all the time – particularly mid-winter when no one wants to take a walk in a snowstorm or late at night!

Scent Remover Spray

Dogs have a fantastic sense of smell. We are talking somewhere between 10,000 and 100,000 times better than yours, depending on the breed. So even if you can't smell their accidents, they certainly still can.

The problem is, while the first time may be an accident, if your dog can still smell their "spot," they might very well keep trying to go to the same place.

Commercial pet scent remover sprays use enzymes to break down biological material, so they can take out smells that your regular detergent just can't. Use them anywhere there has been an "accident" to take away all traces of the scent.

Poop Bags

It is always a good idea to have poop bags with you when you go on a walk (unless you want a hefty fine!), but they are also helpful at home.

Not only does it make cleaning up after your puppy or dog less work later on, but many puppies have a behavioral quirk known as coprophagia. In a nutshell, they eat their own poop. Sometimes, older dogs will also eat puppy poop. Or their own.

Most puppies will outgrow this problem, and in most cases, it is nothing to worry about. Although it might make you queasy!

However, if you pick up the "problem" right away, you won't have to deal with poopy puppy kisses.

Doggy Diapers

Ideally, you want to train your dog to go outside on a schedule and to "ask" when they need to take a walk. However, if you have to be away from home for a while, or your dog has incontinence or "marking" problems, diapers are a big help.

Doggy diapers are available for female dogs (which look like the usual "pants" we are used to) and for male dogs – more of a wrap. There are also washable options for dogs that have ongoing problems.

Treats and Toys.

You know the saying, "you catch more flies with honey?" Well, you train dogs better with treats!

If you can make your dog look forward to their outside time, they will be far more inclined to tell you when they need to go!

Treats as rewards for successful trips to their "business spot" are a good idea for puppies. If you also play together with a special toy when you are outside, they will start to associate being outside for a walk with a pleasant experience. So, they will be far more inclined to let you know when they need to go!

Set Your Dog Up for Success

Getting a new dog is exciting for you, but for a puppy or even an older dog, it can be a stressful experience.

If you are constantly getting angry or upset because they are having accidents around the house, that will only make it harder for them to get used to living with you.

The best way to avoid this is to set your new pupper up for success.

Make sure that you have a plan about the areas you will allow them access to while they are potty training and what's off-limits.

Have the supplies you need on hand before you bring them home, and buy enough to allow for at least a few weeks of training. Whether you have a puppy or an older dog, it is very likely that you're not going to get this figured out in a day or two. So stay consistent, but don't try to rush it.

When you bring a dog home, you are not bringing home a possession. It is a new family member, and your home is now their home too. So, you will have to make some changes so that everyone has what they need to be happy and healthy!

DOGS ARE NOT OUR WHOLE LIFE, BUT THEY MAKE OUR LIVES WHOLE.

- Roger Caras

THREE

Before Training Your Dog

You've heard the saying *"putting the cart before the horse?"* Well, if you haven't already planned how to potty train your dog when you bring him home, you are putting the leash ahead of the dog. *Or something like that!*

Basically, if you don't have a plan, you will spend a lot of time figuring it all out, and it will take longer and be more complicated for the both of you.

If you have stocked up on the supplies and items we mentioned in the last chapter, you are already halfway there. But the stuff is only part of it. You also need to do a little mental preparation and understand a little more about the psychology of dogs.

A dog is one of the most loving beings on the planet. Sharing your life with one is one of the most rewarding things you will ever do. But it is not always easy. There will be times when it will be frustrating, or messy, and even sad. If you are not ready for the emotional and physical responsibility that comes with owning a dog, you should not get one.

When you get a puppy, you are committing ten to fifteen years, at least, to being their guardian, and you can't decide you don't feel like it some days. It is also unfair to a dog or puppy to bring them home and then rehome them later because you aren't ready for the commitment.

If you are not 100% sure that you are ready for all the good, the bad, and the ugly, wait a little while. Owning a dog is a lot like being a parent. It is not for everyone, and it is not a good idea until you are completely ready.

What You Can Expect

Before you try to potty train your dog, you need to get your head in the game, so to speak.

The good news is that potty training dogs goes a lot faster than potty training humans! But it is also not something that happens overnight.

You can expect that there will be the odd accident, but they will become less frequent over time.

You should prepare yourself to face a few messy situations too. For example, there will be times when your puppy's new food does not agree with them or when they have parasites or a tummy bug. It will be gross from time to time, but just like a baby, they depend on you to keep them clean, healthy, and safe. So, make sure you are prepared to do what needs to be done.

Fully potty training your dog (if they are a puppy) will take several weeks to a couple of months at least. But it will get easier as time goes by.

If you are trying to potty train an older dog that you have brought home from a shelter or somewhere else, it could be a quicker process. It all depends on how well trained they were before. Still, it can also take even longer if they have learned bad habits along the way.

This will take patience, but the few weeks you spend on potty training is nothing compared to the many years of unconditional love you are going to get in return. So, try to keep that in mind when you are dealing with surprise puddles!

What You Should Not Expect

Your dog or puppy will learn to do their business where you prefer them to. But they will do it at their own pace. You can plan, prepare, and learn as much as you want to, but your dog is going to do this on their schedule. Not yours.

As much as you might want to set a deadline for this process, don't. If your dog does not meet it, you will only feel disappointed, which isn't worth it.

Don't expect your dog to learn what you expect overnight. Don't expect puppies to make it to their pee pad or outside every time, and remember, when it comes to dogs, poop happens. Even after they are trained!

What Your Dog Wants

What dogs want, more than anything else, is to make their people happy. You can see their joy when you are pleased with them.

This is precisely why scolding them, rubbing their noses in their accidents, and similar punishments don't work. Your dog does not understand why you are unhappy. It just makes them scared and confused.

So as much as you might want to discipline your dog when you step in a surprise puddle, don't.

This is not only true for potty training. It is the basis for your whole relationship with your dog.

Your dog will always want to protect you, to make you happy, and to win your praise and affection. So, if you make a big fuss about the behavior you want to see, they will soon start trying to do more of it.

Patience, Perseverance, and Consistency

Owning a dog is a lot like being a parent. But dogs also behave a lot like kids, and they benefit from many of the same things children do.

Patience is one of the pillars of dog ownership. Your dog will not understand why you are angry about something, and if you react negatively, all you will do is scare them. So, you need to make a conscious effort to stay calm around your dog, whatever happens.

Perseverance is key too. You are not going to get this entirely right the first time. It is going to take time, and there will be mistakes and accidents along the way. The key is not to see these as failures. As long as they're becoming less frequent, you're getting there! Just keep at it!

Finally, there's consistency. Dogs, like children, do best when there is a routine. They like having the same sort of food, at the same time every day. They like to know that they will go out for a walk first thing in the morning and at regular times throughout the day. Dogs like to use the same leash when they go for a walk, and they like going to familiar places.

If you can master all three of these things, you will be a great dog owner, and you will find that everything (not only potty training) is a lot easier for both you and your furry pal.

Now that you know where your head needs to be, and where your dogs is, it's time to look at another key area: myths and old wives' tales about potty training.

OPENING UP YOUR LIFE TO A DOG WHO NEEDS A HOME IS ONE OF THE MOST FULFILLING THINGS YOU CAN DO.

- Emma Kenney

FOUR

Common Myths & Questions

With such easy access to information, you would think that we would be able to find everything we need to know instantly these days. But, unfortunately, the internet and social media are just full of half-truths. When lies and old wives' tales are shared and spread as facts, it can be hard to tell what's really going on and what's true!

So, we have collected some of the most common myths and questions and answered and debunked them for you.

Myth 1: You Need to Show Your Puppy Who's Boss

This is a common myth related to living with a dog. The idea is that you have to establish your dominance in the pack for your dog to respect you. While this might be true with some large, strong dogs like Rottweilers, who arguably need someone with a powerful personality to look up to, most dogs will automatically see you as the leader of your pack.

You do not need to dominate them or make them submit. In fact, if you want to have a loving relationship with your dog, that is precisely what they need: love and kindness.

Myth 2: Rubbing Your Dogs Nose in Their Accident Is Effective

Aside from the fact that, as we have already established, dogs learn far better from positive reinforcement than from discipline, dogs have short attention spans. Puppies even more so.

So, by the time you are rubbing their nose in their puddle, they have probably forgotten they ever did it at all. They don't connect the act of peeing on the rug with your discipline, so they learn nothing. The only thing this achieves is to confuse and upset your puppy.

In fact, if you use negative reinforcement like this, you are only likely to make your puppy try to "hide" their accidents. So, if they do need to go when you're not around, they might find a hidden corner to do it in so that they don't get punished. That just means you will have stinky corners in your home!

Myth 3: Your Puppy Did It Deliberately

Some people believe that puppies deliberately misbehave. This is not true.

Your puppy's behavior is no less deliberate than a human baby. Neither one of them is doing the things you don't like to spite you. They just don't know better, or they might not be able to help themselves.

Myth 4: Your Puppy Will Outgrow It

Some people think that your puppy will outgrow all their problems in time if you just leave them to it.

This is not true. Your dog may learn things on their own as they grow up, but when it comes to the behavior you want to avoid or encourage, it is up to you to steer them in the right direction.

Your puppy will not learn appropriate toilet practices if you don't train them, and if they learn bad habits early on, you will have a tough time trying to change them.

Myth 5: Some Breeds Can't Be Trained

This is absolutely not true. Some breeds are generally more intelligent and can be easier to train, but no dog breed can't be trained at all. This is especially true when it comes to the basics, like potty training!

Some people also think that some breeds, like small breeds, can't be toilet trained. This is also not true. Every dog can be taught to do their business where you want them to.

Myth 6: You Can't Potty Train Older Dogs

Many people believe that if you adopt an older dog with less than fantastic toilet habits, you are stuck with it. But this is also not true. It is harder to potty train older dogs, but it is not impossible. Prepare for a long process, and make sure you have backup plans like a crate for when you are not around or diapers if you don't have one!

Myth 7: Your Puppy Will Show You When They Need to Go

This is not true. Older dogs who are already potty trained might let you know that they need to go out, but puppies generally don't.

Very young puppies typically won't even sniff around before they need to go. In fact, they probably don't even realize that they need to!

It is best to try to take your puppy out a few minutes after they eat and regularly throughout the day. If your puppy has the opportunity to do their business before they even realize they need to, you will have far fewer accidents! Although some minor clues might let you know it's about to go down, these are unique signals different for every dog.

Myth 8: Dogs Always "Go" When They Go Outside

This is not true – especially with puppies! Your backyard or outside area is an exciting place, full of new smells, things to explore. Also, this is even without mentioning the exciting possibility of spotting a bird or a squirrel. Your puppy might be so distracted by all that excitement that they forget to go. So always stay with them and watch that they actually get the job done before you head inside.

Potty Training Questions and Answers

Now that we have dispelled some of the most common myths out there, it is time to get to the top questions and answers you need.

How Old Should My Puppy Be to Potty Train?

You would not try to potty train a human baby before they are ready, and the same is true for dogs.

Puppies that are too young simply will not understand what you are trying to achieve. You should not bring a puppy into your home until they are about 8 to 10 weeks, but they won't be able to potty train until they are about 12 to 16 weeks. So, you will have a few weeks of pee pads to deal with before you get started!

Do Puppies Have Bladder Control?

Not really. Puppies will go as soon as they feel uncomfortable. Whether that means pee or a bowel movement. Their bladders are tiny, too, so that happens a lot more frequently than you think! This is why we recommend taking them outside every hour or so, even if you don't think they need to, and after every meal.

Do Crates Always Work?

Crates are a great way to help prevent accidents, particularly for short periods of time. But, while your puppy will try not to take a bathroom break where he or she sleeps, they might still go in a corner if there is too much room. This is why it's a good idea to have a smaller, puppy-sized crate while you puppy train, and then graduate to a larger one once they've got the hang of their new routine.

How Long Should Your Puppy Be in Their Crate?

As we have already mentioned, puppies have tiny bladders. Which means that they need to go to the bathroom every hour or two. Older dogs can "hold it" overnight or for several hours at a time, but puppies just can't.

Your puppy's crate should be a temporary solution when you can't be around to take them out. They should have a larger space with a pee pad that they can use at night. They might have a few accidents, but they will soon learn that the pee pad is an acceptable bathroom option!

Can My Puppy Just Use the Doggy Door?

A doggy door is a great idea – for older dogs, who know that they are supposed to go outside, and how to get there.

But while you can show your puppy where it is and how to use it, they will not be able to take themselves out to pee for a while. As we have already mentioned, they might not even know they need to for a while!

I Take My Puppy Out Every Hour, and They Still Have Accidents?

Once an hour is a good rule of thumb to start with, but some puppies may need to go more often, especially when they are very young. If you are still finding puddles when taking them out every hour, try every forty minutes or even every half hour. Of course, the time will increase as they get older, but when puppies are very young, a big part of their day is bathroom breaks!

Why Does My Puppy Seem to Seek Out the Carpet?

Older puppies, who might already be getting used to going outside, might find that your carpets feel a lot like grass. Since you are happy when they go on grass, they might assume the carpet is a good spot too.

When your puppy is very young, if you can, it's a good idea to keep them away from carpets, to avoid the confusion!

How Long Will My Puppy Take to Go?

Many people find that their puppy will have an accident immediately after coming in from a trip outside. The simple answer is you didn't wait long enough. It may take five or ten minutes, but make sure that they do go before you head back indoors.

Do Older Puppies Still Have Accidents?

Yes. While they have more control than younger puppies, older puppies and dogs can still have "accidents" if they need to and can't or don't want to go out.

A good example of this is a mostly potty-trained older pup who doesn't want to go out when it is raining or snowing. Sometimes, even if they know how to get out, you will still have to make sure they actually do.

My Older Puppy or Dog Is Having Frequent Accidents in My House. Why?

As we have mentioned before, sometimes, accidents are due to medical conditions. This could be something as simple as a bladder infection or something more serious. If you notice that a dog or puppy that has been potty trained for some time is having frequent accidents, speak to your vet.

Know Your Sources

As you can see, there are lots of questions and myths about potty training dogs and puppies out there.

Hopefully, these have answered some of them for you, but if you still need more information, make sure you get it from a credible source.

Your veterinarian is an excellent person to ask, as is anyone who is a dog trainer or behavior specialist. However, be cautious about the advice you get on social media and similar. Even the most well-meaning people sometimes spread incorrect information.

Now that we've got that out of the way, it's time to talk food and poop.

MY FASHION PHILOSOPHY IS, IF YOU'RE NOT COVERED IN DOG HAIR, YOUR LIFE IS EMPTY.

- Elayne Boosler

FIVE

Dog Food & Poop

Any new parent (*of a dog or a human*) will tell you that they never imagined they would have so many conversations and thoughts about poop. It is not pretty, but it is true!

However, while human babies mostly have bottles for the first six months, you are going to start feeding your new puppy dog food as soon as they arrive. Sometimes, that food will not agree with them, and you will find that out pretty quickly!

Puppies have sensitive tummies. They also have tiny teeth that can't really cope with hard foods, and they don't really know when to stop. All of that adds up to potentially explosive situations!

So, before you find out the hard way the role food plays in poop, read on, and take preventative actions!

Find Out What They Are Eating

If you are a first-time dog owner, you might not know this, but changing a dog's food can result in tummy trouble, even if the food itself is good for them.

It is always a good idea to ask the breeder, shelter, or store that you got your puppy from what they have been eating and get some of that food for them.

Even if you plan to change their food, you should mix them together for a few days or weeks, gradually increasing the ratio of new food to old. Making the change suddenly will almost certainly result in an upset stomach!

Puppies Don't Know When They Are Full

The next thing you need to know is that puppies don't really know what full is or how to recognize when they are! We have all seen puppies with fat little bellies after they stuffed themselves with food, and it is cute. But it will also result in some toilet trouble.

Make sure that you're feeding younger puppies smaller meals more frequently to ensure that they aren't overeating.

As you know, being too full makes you feel uncomfortable, and it can lead to other problems.

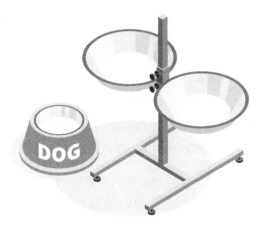

Dog Food Basics

There are many dog food brands out there today that market their products based on meat content and being grain-free. They use pictures of wolves and similar on their bags, and it all sounds pretty good.

However, there are potentially life-threatening conditions like Canine dilated cardiomyopathy or DCM, which have been linked to feeding grain-free diets. We are not going to get into that here. Still, the best dog foods are the ones that meet WSAVA guidelines. There are five major brands that meet these: Purina, Iams, Eukanuba, Hills Science Diet, and Royal Canin.

These brands have been formulated by veterinary nutritionists and undergone rigorous studies over many years. There are many options in all of their lines, including budget-friendly brands and prescription diets, so there's something for everyone.

Speak to your vet about which kind of food is best for your dog but remember that grain-free does not mean good for them!

Some owners also choose to make their own dog food. This can be a great option if you know what you are doing and follow some guidelines.

The Importance of Proper Nutrition

Many dog owners make the mistake of thinking that feeding their dogs "human foods" means they love them more. But, while they might have the best intentions, this can actually do a lot more harm than good. There are several things you need to know about dog nutrition, but here are the basics:

- Human food is too rich and contains many ingredients that can be harmful to dogs.
- Rich human food can cause potentially fatal conditions like pancreatitis.
- Obesity is just as dangerous for dogs as it is for humans. Without a balanced diet formulated for dogs, it is easy for your dog to gain too much weight.
- Dog foods formulated for puppies are not just smaller than adult food. They are specially formulated with more calories and protein, etc., to support all the growing your dog is doing!
- Most dog food bags have feeding guidelines on them that are based on weight. Make sure you weigh your dog from time to time to ensure you are feeding them the right amount.
- Some dogs have food sensitivities and allergies, but these can be hard to diagnose without an elimination diet. If your dog is having tummy trouble, speak to your vet. They can probably recommend a food with a protein like salmon or lamb that is easier to digest.
- Only ever feed your dog-approved and safe dog treats!

Along with properly formulated food, all your dog needs is fresh, clean water. Dogs do not need milk, and cows' milk can easily trigger tummy trouble – even in puppies!

Human Foods That Are Dangerous for Dogs

Sometimes, your dog will have gastrointestinal symptoms even if you have not fed them something they should not have had. Dogs and puppies can be very sneaky, though, and they do love human food! So an accidental nibble of certain human foods isn't out of the realm of possibilities. Inadvertent eating of that foods can at times be a cause for a medical emergency, so if you suspect your dog has had any of these, go to the vet right away:

- Chocolate, especially dark chocolate
- Onions and garlic
- Sugar-free gum or any product with the artificial sweetener Xylitol
- Grapes and raisins
- Fruit pips and seeds, including cherry pits and apple seeds.
- Alcohol
- Coffee and tea (and any other caffeinated beverages)
- Avocados
- Macadamia nuts
- Salt
- Tomato and rhubarb leaves and stems
- Bread dough (not toxic, but can "rise" inside the gut, causing a blockage)

Tiny amounts of these foods, in some cases, won't do severe or permanent damage. But even just a few pieces of gum, for instance, can be fatal.

If your dog has eaten something they should not have, always seek medical attention as soon as possible. This is NOT the time for a wait-and-see approach!

Quality Food Makes Quality Poops

Yes. You are going to start rating your dog's poop. You never thought you would be here, but this is part of being a pet owner!

The good news is that quality dog food will result in small, compact, less smelly, and never loose poops that are easier to clean up. This means even if they have the occasional accident indoors, you will not have to send the rugs to the incinerator!

If your dog is not eating the right kind of food, their stools may be looser, smellier, and bulkier.

Pay attention to your dog's stools. They will tell you if your dog might have an allergy or sensitivity, or if you might need to try another type of food.

Dog Poops and Health

As gross as it seems, an animal's stool can tell you a lot about their health. Aside from just paying attention to the consistency of your dog's stools, you should also look for any health warnings they might be giving you. These could include:

- Bloody stools. A small amount of blood occasionally is not cause to panic. Still, if you see more than one or two in a row or a lot of blood, you need to speak to your veterinarian as soon as possible.
- Very dark, almost black stools are also a warning sign. This might be a sign of old blood somewhere in the intestine, which could be something serious.
- Straining very hard. This could be constipation, which could be related to dehydration, but it could also be a sign of blockage. This could be serious and may require veterinary intervention.

- Very loose stools with sudden onset are usually a sign of infection. This could be bacterial or viral, and while many clear up on their own, some, like parvovirus, can be fatal if not treated.
- Mucous or signs of parasites mean that your dog needs to be dewormed. Intestinal parasites, left untreated, can be very dangerous for your dog.
- White stools usually mean that your dog is getting too much calcium.
- Greasy poops mean that your dog is getting more fat than they need.

There are many other things that your dog's poop could be telling you, but the simple rule is that if things have changed suddenly, there is a problem somewhere. Never try to self-diagnose or treat a poop problem yourself. Many of these conditions can be dangerous or even deadly. You need to speak to a trained veterinarian as soon as possible.

Dogs Are What They Eat Too!

We always say that people are what they eat, and that is true of dogs too.

But dogs need different things than humans, and feeding them foods we like can be very dangerous.

A good rule of thumb is that your dog should get 90% of their nutrition from a good quality dog food, and the other 10% can be treats and snacks. (But again, stick to the doggy type – human food can be horrible for dogs!)

Your dog's poop is kind of like a crystal ball. It will tell you if there is something wrong. While you don't have to obsess about it, it is always a good idea to pay attention. Some severe conditions can come on suddenly, and without treatment, could be very dangerous for your dog.

NO MATTER HOW LITTLE MONEY AND HOW FEW POSSESSIONS YOU OWN, HAVING A DOG MAKES YOU RICH.

- Louis Sabin

Training

Every dog is unique. But just like you can count on human nature to predict how most people will act, dogs all act and react in similar ways in similar situations. Some may be more docile and others more excitable, but there are certain common traits that every dog will share.

This is good news because it means that training strategies that work for one dog will probably work for others, although it may take more or less time. Some dogs learn very quickly, while others need more time. But if you follow proven training strategies, eventually, you will get the results you want.

Do try to remember, though, that dogs will be dogs, and we can't expect them to behave the way we want them to. We can teach them what we want, but ultimately, they are going to act like dogs. They will all sniff other dog's butts, and they are all going to lick their own butts and do all the other doggy things.

If you can't handle those things, then maybe it is not the best time to become a dog owner!

Scheduling

Schedule's work. They work for successful adults who do the same things at the same time every day. They work for kids. And they work very well for dogs.

Dogs are creatures of habit. Doing the same things at roughly the same times makes them feel safe. They like to have the same kind of food every day, have their bed in the same place, and play with their favorite toys every day.

This is why, when you are moving, your dog probably seems stressed. Their routine is out of whack, and they don't know how to cope.

This is good news for dog owners because routines and schedules are the basis of training. If your dog knows that they are supposed to do certain things at certain times and in predefined ways, they will do the same thing every time. You can work with this and figure out a schedule that works for you and your dog.

Puppy Schedules

Puppies are different from adult dogs in the same ways that human babies are different from adults. Just like babies need to sleep more, eat more, and go to the bathroom more often, your puppy does too.

So, you need to have a different schedule for your puppy than you will when they are adults.

Your puppy will need to eat more frequently at first than they will later on. This will probably look a little like this:

- Most puppies need to have three meals a day – breakfast, lunch, and dinner. This may vary based on things like their food, breed, and so on. Always follow the guidelines on your dog food bag unless your vet recommends something else.

- You probably want to take your puppy out for a toilet break when they wake up and then give them breakfast shortly after that.
- Immediately after they eat, they should go outside too. Food and water tend to move through all babies pretty quickly, and puppies are no different!
- Every half hour to hour, your puppy should go outside for a potty break – even if they are not sniffing around. They won't always give you a warning when they need to go!
- Your puppy should also go out before they go to bed. If you are not taking them out at night, make sure they have a pee pad that is accessible and that they know where it is.

Of course, as you can see, this kind of schedule is very hands-on. If you cannot be with your puppy every day, you might want to hire a "sitter" or find a doggy daycare that can stick to the schedule when you are at work. Be warned, though, this can be tricky. Many daycare facilities don't accept dogs that aren't fully vaccinated, so you might need to hire someone to go to your home until your puppy is.

Adult Dog Schedules

Older dogs can "hold it" for many hours at a time, under normal circumstances. Unless there is a medical condition that prevents them to, they should be able to sleep through an entire night without needing to go.

But adult dogs still benefit from a schedule.

It is a good idea to take your dog out every morning, at lunchtime, and before bed.

Older dogs usually also "ask" to go out when they need to, and it is a good idea to listen when they do! You can't blame your pooch if you don't take them out, and they can't hold it! However, it may become a habit over time, so make sure you clean up carefully and next time, when they ask, listen!

Trial and Error

Finding a routine that works for you and your dog won't happen immediately. It will take a while before you figure out precisely what kind of schedule works best for your puppy or dog, and it might change over time.

Puppies usually need to eat more often and take more bathroom breaks. Older dogs less so, but elderly dogs might again need to go out more frequently as their bladder control falters a little.

You will probably also find that if you get another dog, the schedule changes a little too, as you try to balance different ages, stages, and needs.

Give It Time

When you first bring a new dog home, whether it is a puppy or an older rescue, their whole lives just changed in an instant.

A puppy will have just left their mom and their brother's and sisters. They will be confused, and a little afraid, and they might not know what is happening.

An older dog that has been adopted or rescued might have been through a lot. They might be used to a kennel, and they might not trust that this new home is a permanent one.

That is a lot for them to deal with, and it will take time before they get past all their confusion and concern. So, it is no wonder that it might take a while before they figure it all out.

Potty training your new dog will take time. How long? No one can say for sure.

Most dogs will get the general idea within a few weeks or a couple of months, but some may need more time. You can't set a start and end date for this process, as much as you might want to. It is going to take as long as it takes, and you can't rush it.

So, try to be patient and relax. Your dog will know if you are stressed out, and it will only make everything take that much longer.

Expect Slip-Ups

A lot of people think that training a dog is a linear process. That you will start at point A, work through various things, and your dog will become incrementally better trained until you get to point B. They think that it is always going to be a case of growth in the right direction. But the truth is, that is not how it works.

Dogs, like people, have good days and bad days. You might not have had an accident happen in weeks or even months, and then one day, you find a puddle with your foot. This is entirely normal, and it does not mean that your dog has forgotten everything they learned!

It is usually just because they got distracted and forgot what they had learned. Or maybe, it was particularly rainy outside, and your dog just really didn't want to face it. That happens too. It is important not to overreact. Make sure you clean the spot well, and for a couple of days, shorten the period between their outside time.

Also, watch for signs of illness. Sometimes, potty accidents result from an illness or undiagnosed condition, and if it happens frequently, it is worth discussing with your veterinarian.

Potty Schedules by Age

Dogs have different bathroom break needs at different ages. If you are home all the time to take them out, this is not really a factor, but if you have to go out to work or for other reasons, you might need to find a way to stop home during the day or hire a person or company that offers this service.

The following table provides general information about how often dogs need to go outside at various ages:

AGE	BATHROOM BREAK FREQUENCY
2 Months	At least every two hours, but possibly more often
3 Months	At least every four hours
4 Months	At least every five hours
5 Months	At least every six hours
7 Months	At least every eight hours

It is also worth noting that smaller dogs typically need to go outside more frequently since their bladders are smaller. Older dogs will also need to go outside more often than young adults.

If you can't meet this kind of schedule, consider hiring someone who can stop by your house to let your dogs out, or create an indoor "toilet" area with pee pads and similar.

Feeding Schedules

Like human babies, puppies tend to need to have a bowel movement within about a half an hour of having a meal (sometimes less). So, feeding times are an essential part of your schedule and planning.

Even older dogs will usually need to go out within an hour or so of having a meal, so it's a good idea to factor that into your daily schedule too.

Puppies usually have three meals a day, so make sure you keep them around the same time and take your puppy out or to their toilet area about fifteen minutes after eating. Wait for them to do what they need to, and you should avoid any smelly accidents.

If you go out to work or study and you have an older dog, you should also try to feed your dog as soon as you get up so that there's enough time for them to digest the meal and take a walk before you leave.

Keeping meals at regular times is vital at all ages and stages of your dog's life, so make a schedule, and stick to it!

DOGS ARE OUR LINK TO PARADISE.

- Milan Kundera

Strategies

You know the old saying, "failing to plan is planning to fail?" That is true about dog training too.

While potty training is undoubtedly the most basic type of dog training you are likely to do, it is still good to have a plan in mind. You might find that you don't follow it all the way through the process or that things change over time. That is perfectly normal too.

There are various factors that can impact your dog's potty training, including your schedule, where you live (a house or an apartment, for instance), and other things.

In this chapter, we look at several options you might want to consider when potty training your dog. But as always, since both you and your dog are individuals, you should tailor these to your needs.

You may find that a hybrid model works best or that you need to change your potty-training strategy when you move to a new home or change jobs. Some people even have different methods based on the seasons. Because let's face it. No one wants to go outside when it is extremely cold or very rainy!

These are a few of the strategies you have that you can use to get your sweet pupper potty trained.

Option 1:

Aim for Outside

If you have one puppy and you are always around to watch them, it may be worth aiming to always get them to "go" outside.

As we have mentioned before, this is more than just looking for them to show signs that they are considering a spot to do their business. Very young puppies might not give you any warning before they make a puddle on the rug!

If you plan to try to get them to "go" outside all the time during the day, set an alarm on your phone or similar for every half hour. Then whether they "ask" to go or not, take them outside and stay with them until they do their business.

You will still have to have a designated potty area in their sleeping space if you try this method, but as time goes by and their bladder and bowel control works better, you will find you have less cleaning up to do.

Pros of the Always Outside Method

- Your puppy will quickly begin to associate outside with their toilet time.
- There will be less cleanup for you to do (provided you get your timing right!)
- If the weather is nice, you also get to spend time outside with your puppy!
- There will be fewer spaces in your home that will smell like your puppy's "toilet," so there will be less confusion as they get older.

Cons of the Always Outside Method

- This method is very hands-on and takes a lot of commitment, particularly early on.
- You need to be around all the time if you choose to toilet train your puppy this way.
- If you get a puppy in the winter, you will be spending a lot of time in the snow or rain.

Option 2:

<u>Inside Potty Only</u>

If you have a tiny dog or live in an area where you don't have a fenced yard or there is often extreme weather, you might find that training your dog to do their business inside all the time is the best option.

Pee pads and fake grass mats are great for this but remember that you should always put them on a tray with sides, so any liquid won't leak. Also, remember that when male dogs get older, they will still lift their legs, so any walls, chair legs, or curtains near their pee pad might get peed on! There are special indoor pee options for male dogs that might work for you.

If you plan to potty train your dog to go inside, choose a spot in your home that is out of the way, easy for them to access, and easy to clean.

While your puppy is little, you might want to use a portable fence to close the area off, and since they will need to "go" during the night, place their sleeping basket or crate in the same area.

Pros of the Inside Potty Only Method

- If you live in a townhouse or apartment, where your dog will probably be using an indoor potty all the time, it makes sense to train them this way.
- This method is ideal for tiny dogs, who might not be able to go outside unaccompanied, particularly in winter.
- This is a convenient option for dogs and owners.

Cons of the Inside Potty Only Method

- Things can get stinky and messy fast!
- If you don't invest in pee pads and use newspapers instead, your dog might be trained to think all newspapers are potties!
- If your dog gets used to going inside, it can be hard to break the habit later.
- If you are not very careful, smells can get into flooring, walls, or furniture, which can encourage your dog to use those areas again in the future.

Option 3:

Isolated Areas Method

If your dog will be using a pee pad or "fake grass" style of indoor "toilet," you will find that they can get confused between their pee pad and your carpets.

The best way to avoid that confusion (and since your pup will assume anywhere that smells like "them" is a suitable spot to go) is to keep them away from areas with rugs or carpets.

Create a toilet zone for your dog that is easy to clean and will not soak up smells.

Remove rugs from your home to prevent confusion and limit their access to areas that have fitted carpets until they are used to their "spot."

If you choose to teach your puppy to "go" in an indoor toilet spot, you will still need to take them to the area when they need to go. So, make sure you or someone you can trust is around all the time to take them to their toilet!

Pros of the Isolated Areas Method

- A designated indoor "toilet" area in your home means you don't have to brave nasty weather.
- Removing confusing rugs and limiting access to carpeted areas means cleanup will be easier when there are accidents.
- As your dog gets older, you can keep their "bathroom" in the same place, and they will always know where to go.

Cons of the Isolated Areas Method

- If your dog learns to go to the bathroom inside, it may be hard to change the habit later on.

- You will need to clean their toilet area every day for as long as they "go" inside.
- If you have more than one dog using an indoor toilet area, it can get stinky fast!
- You will need to invest in good pee pads, which can get expensive over time.

Option 4:

The Little Bit Closer Method

If you want to start your dog off on pee pads in the house when they are little but gradually transition them to going outdoors, you can use a "mobile" pee pad lined tray to get them used to going on the pee pad, regardless of location.

Over time, you can move the tray closer and closer to the door or exit that they will eventually use to get outside.

If you do try this method, it is essential to make sure that whatever you put your pee pads in will not leak. If your whole house smells like puppy "accidents," it's going to be very hard to clean, for one thing. For another, if your dog smells their "business" everywhere, they won't know for sure where they need to go.

Eventually, they will get used to going on that particular tray, so even when you move it outside, they might continue using it for a while.

Pros of the Little Bit Closer Method

- You can start potty training your dog indoors, which is great if the weather is not fantastic.
- Your puppy will start to associate their pee pad and tray with going to the bathroom, so they will look for that rather than just sniffing around for a spot they went before.
- With a pee pad in a leak-proof container, you can easily clean up messes when necessary.
- Eventually, you can move their pee pad and tray outside, and they can use the door or doggie door to get to it. Then, when they are used to going in the yard, you can remove the pee pad tray altogether.

Cons of the Little Bit Closer Method

- There will be a lot of daily cleanups as you work your way closer to the outdoors!
- Even when you do get your dog to "go" outside, you will have to break the habit of using their pee pad tray.

Option 5:

The Hired Gun

If you can't be home with your puppy all the time, it will be a lot harder to get your pup potty trained. The best option, in this case, is to hire someone to help, either in your home or at a separate location. Dog sitters and doggie daycares are an excellent option for young puppies if you can't be home with them. Still, you may not be able to take them to a "social" setting with other puppies until they have had all their shots.

While this may sound like an inconvenience, some severe illnesses might be spread in settings like this that can be dangerous or even deadly for puppies. If a daycare does not demand that all their visitors are vaccinated, it is probably not a safe place for your puppy.

One option to get around this is to use a dog sitter in your home until they have had their vaccinations and then move them to a doggie daycare. The added bonus of the latter is that they will also get socialized at the same time!

Pros of the Hired Gun Method

- A great choice for working dog parents who can't be with their puppy all the time.
- If your dog is in daycare, several people will be around to help with training.
- Professional dog caregivers are usually trained and have the skills to train your puppy.
- If your dog goes to a daycare, they will be socialized while perfecting their potty training.

Cons of the Hired Gun Method

- Doggy daycares are not available for very young puppies, so you will need to make other arrangements until they have all their shots.
- The cost of professional dog care can be relatively high.

- Your dog can pick up both good and bad habits in doggy daycare!

Option 6:

Doggie Diapers

If you are trying to potty train an older dog with bad toilet habits, you might find that they are hard to break.

Doggy diapers can help prevent messes and smells while you get your dog used to the idea that they need to go where you want them to.

There are diapers available for male and female dogs, and they are easy to use. There are also washable and disposable options available. Note, however, that diapers are designed for pee rather than solids. So, you might still have unwanted surprises!

Pros of the Doggy Diaper Method

- Doggy diapers are a great backup plan if you have an older dog who might sneak off to pee where they aren't supposed to.
- Diapers are also great for older dogs that might not have the bladder control they used to.
- If your dog is tough to train, diapers can be a

long-term solution for times when you can't be around to watch them and take them out.

Cons of the Doggy Diaper Method

- Many dogs learn how to remove their diapers. Once they do, you can't be sure they will stay where you put them.
- If your dog gets used to being able to pee at will, you aren't really training them. You are just making cleanup easier!
- Doggy diapers can be expensive over time.

Teach Your Dog to Ask!

When your puppy is very young, they're just going to need to go out as often as possible. But as their bladders get a little bigger and they gain more control, it is good to teach them to ask when they need to go outside.

If you notice that your puppy is whining at the door, scratching on the floor near the door, or otherwise trying to signal you that they need to go outside, take them!

Sometimes, they will just want to play or chase a rabbit, but usually, they will also go to the bathroom.

This is something you cannot really "teach," as it happens naturally if you are consistent with taking them outside for their pee breaks. When they feel the urge, they will want to go where they are used to going to relieve themselves.

If your dog learns that they can trust you to take them out when they need to go, they will be sure to let you know when they need to go. Some dogs will even come and find you when they need to go for a walk, which is a great way to prevent accidents in your house!

Mixed Methods

The fact is, there is no one size fits all way to toilet train a dog or puppy because there are no one size fits all families!

Some people are happy to let smaller dogs do their business inside their home, perhaps in a basement or a covered porch. Others, particularly when they have more than one dog or larger breed dogs, need them to learn to go outside.

Some people work full time, so they have to find someone else to help with potty training, while others might have kids or a family member who can help.

Sometimes, temporary measures like nighttime pee pads or diapers for accidents are a good idea. Still, some people prefer to just set a timer and do regular trips outside while their puppy or dog is learning.

The best idea is to think about these things before you ever bring a dog or puppy home so that you can decide if there is a workable option. You should never bring a dog or puppy home if you don't want to have to deal with things like potty training. You can't avoid this, and if you get angry or frustrated, it is just not fair to the dog.

There is no hard and fast rule for potty training your dog or puppy. No one can tell you that taking them out every half hour will mean no accidents or that diapers will work for them. But what we can guarantee is that with time and patience, you will get there eventually. You may need to modify your initial plan to find what works, and you may need to ask for help along the way. But it is always worth it to take the time to get your new bestie used to your home and to avoid nasty cold, wet spots on the rug!

Now that you know some basic strategies you might be able to accommodate to get your dog potty trained, it is time to look at what to do when things don't go according to plan.

BE THE PERSON YOUR DOG THINKS YOU ARE.

- C.J. Frick

Solutions

Planning is great. It will give you something to start with. But ask anyone who has shared their life with a puppy or dog, and they will tell you that dogs are not great at following plans!

Part of the charm of having a dog in your life is that they are unique, funny, and entertaining beings with minds of their own. Which makes them part of the family but also makes it a little challenging to get them to do what you want them to sometimes.

The good news is that dogs naturally want to please their people. So eventually, they will work out what makes you happy and do more of that. But in the meantime, it is a good idea to have a plan for when things don't go according to, well, plan.

This chapter is all about how you should handle the problems that will invariably arise as you go through the process of potty training your new buddy. So, make notes, stock up on supplies, and make sure your patience is set to maximum!

Expect the Unexpected

The first thing you need to do as a new dog owner is to get your mindset right when it comes to potty training and everything else.

A dog or puppy is not a toy or a robot. They are going to do things that are weird, annoying, frustrating, and messy. You will have chewed shoes, the occasional puddle, and a lifetime of stinky dog farts to deal with.

Expect craziness. Learn to love chasing your dog when he or she takes off unexpectedly and know that life with a dog is perfect because it is not.

If you are not ready to deal with a little bit of chaos in your life, you should not be planning to add a puppy to your life, never mind figuring out how to potty train them.

So, if perfection is more important than family, and a little disorder makes you crazy, give it a few years before you consider getting a dog again. It will take time, there will be smells, noises, and the odd bit of destruction. Still, in return, you will get a lifetime of perfectly imperfect devotion.

Dealing with Accidents

They say the only two things in life that are certain are death and taxes. But you can add another one to that list. Puppies will have accidents.

Even older dogs cannot "hold it" indefinitely, and if they're stuck inside for too long, they will have to "go" eventually.

So, no matter how careful and attentive you are, you will be dealing with accidents from time to time. The good news is that cleaning them up and preventing future occurrences is not too hard.

- If you are potty training a puppy or have an older dog and you have to go out for an extended time, make sure they are in a part of the house that is easy to clean. Tile and vinyl flooring are a lot easier to clean up than carpet or hardwood floors!

- Have an emergency pee pad in your living space if you are potty training your puppy, even if you plan to have them go outside. You can't always make it all the way out if you see them getting ready to make a puddle, but at least you can try to get them to a pee pad!

- If you have a puppy or dog that is not fully trained, try to limit the places they can access and check for accidents frequently. The sooner you can clean them up, the less chance there is of permanent damage or stains.

- Mop up any liquid from carpets and floors, as well as any solids.

- Clean the area with an appropriate household cleaner to help prevent staining.

- Once the area is dry, use an enzyme-based pet odor spray to completely remove the smell of urine or feces from the area. Dogs tend to "go" where they have gone before, and other dogs might also want to "mark" the site of any accidents. Enzyme sprays help to take the smell away completely. But remember – just because you can't smell it, does not mean your dog can't!

As we have already mentioned, punishing your dog for accidents is pointless. Unless you catch them in the act, they probably won't even remember they did it. Particularly if they are puppies!

Do not try to discipline a dog or puppy for an accident. Instead, use it as a learning experience – *for you*! What caused them to have an accident? Do you need to take them out more frequently? Was it right after a meal? Should you restrict access to that part of the house?

Accidents will happen. That is guaranteed. But they will become less frequent and easier to avoid overtime. So, take them in stride, and adjust your potty-training plan accordingly.

Corrective Training

Rubbing your puppy's nose in their puddles is about as effective as rubbing your own. But that doesn't mean there aren't things you can do to help steer them in the right direction. The trick is to catch them before the damage is done!

This is why it's so important to make sure you're always around when your puppy is wandering and that they're limited to a relatively small area.

Puppies don't always sniff around looking for a place to pee, particularly when they are very young. Still, there are some signs that show they might be thinking of taking a potty break. If they become very still or squat or hunch slightly, things might get messy soon!

The best way to break this behavior is to use a loud noise to interrupt them. Clapping your hands or saying "outside" loudly might be all it takes to break their concentration and give you time to get them outside or to their emergency pee pad. If you plan to use a whistle or a clicker for training, later, you might also want to start training with them when your dog is still a puppy.

Even if you have to use this tactic, it's essential to give your puppy lots of praise when they "finish the job" in the right place. Positive reinforcement is the best training tool you have. Dogs want to please their people, so they will always try to do more of the things that make you happy, and that cause you to praise them and give them lots of attention!

Health Issues

Being a dog parent is a lot like being a parent to a human. You're going to spend a lot more time thinking about poop and everything bathroom-related than you ever thought possible.

There are several things your puppy or dog's bathroom behavior can tell you about their health, and it pays to pay attention.

Parasite Problems

Many puppies have parasites (usually what we call worms.) Sometimes, you can spot these in their poop, or sometimes, they do things like drag their butts on the carpet. Your puppy should be getting a dewormer when they go to the veterinarian for their vaccinations, but if you notice problems in between visits, it is worth making a call or paying them a visit, just to be sure.

Internal parasites, left untreated, can cause a lot of problems, and many can be transferred between your dog and the humans in your family too.

Loose Stools

Puppies usually eat softer food, particularly when they are very young. It makes sense that if it goes in softer, it'll come out the same way.

But once your dog graduates to harder, more adult-like food, you should notice a change in their stools.

If your puppy has frequent, loose stools, it could be a sign of a problem and might need medical attention. Likewise, if your puppy's stools are a weird color. Very light, very dark, or spotted with blood or mucous are all causes for concern.

Watch for signs of dehydration and listlessness, but if a puppy has more than one or two very loose stools in a row, it is probably time for a trip to the vet.

Urination Trouble

Just like people, you can tell a lot about your dog's health by their urine. Yes, I know the last thing you ever imagined doing was examining dog pee. Welcome to the world of dog parenting.

Puppies have tiny bladders, so they pee a lot. Sometimes as frequently as every half hour – or even more often! But as they grow older, they should learn to control their bladders a little more. If your dog is several months old and still peeing a lot, there might be something else wrong that needs attention. Other urine related issues you need to watch out for are:

- Not urinating often enough. This can be a sign of dehydration, which is often a symptom of a severe health condition.
- Urine that is a strange color. This might be easier to spot on a pee pad.
- Urine that smells particularly strong. Again, this might be a sign of dehydration.
- Dribbling urine or needing to urinate soon after they have been outside. This could be a sign of a bladder or kidney infection.

- Straining to urinate or trying and not being able to.

No one wants to spend too much time thinking about these things, and no one ever tells you that it will be part of owning a dog. But your dog or puppy can't tell you when something is not right, and paying attention to things like this will help you tell when a trip to the veterinarian is needed.

Dogs can get conditions like diabetes and kidney stones, and these and many other conditions have symptoms related to urination. Spotting these problems early and getting treatment can help ensure that your dog enjoys a longer, healthier life.

Territorial Peeing

Whether we like it or not, dogs are territorial animals. It is why they bark when someone comes in your yard or when someone comes too close when you are out.

Dogs are also pack animals, but in the modern world, the pack looks a little different. Instead of a dozen wolves running across the tundra, you have three or four humans, a dog or two, and maybe a cat. That does not mean that dogs will not still act like their wild ancestors, and territory marking is one of those things.

Male dogs, particularly those that aren't neutered, are far more likely to want to mark their territory than females. This might be an ongoing problem, or it might be triggered by a disruption in their lives. Like adding a new pet or baby to the family or even moving to a new house.

Sometimes, particularly when a smaller, older dog starts to worry about their place in the pack when a puppy starts growing a lot bigger than them, they will try to assert themselves by marking territory.

If you have ever seen a tiny male dog nearly fall over trying to pee higher on a tree than a bigger, younger male, you know exactly how this plays out.

Even when you go on walks with a male dog, they probably want to stop every five minutes to check their "pee-mail" on a tree and leave a message of their own.

There isn't much you can do about this behavior except try to prevent it in the house. Take extra precautions to avoid accidents inside. If they do happen, clean them immediately and thoroughly, and use an enzyme spray to remove as much of the scent as possible.

Try to establish a routine in your "pack" and treat each dog as an individual. Make sure that everyone gets enough attention, too – especially if you have had some sort of upheaval in your lives.

Food Allergies

If your dog is having frequent poop accidents, it may be because they have a sensitivity to something in their food. Just like humans, some dogs are sensitive or even allergic to things in their food and their environment.

Unfortunately, just like humans, it is nearly impossible to figure out what the trigger for an allergic or intolerance reaction is with testing because there are so many things it could be.

If your dog is having a nasty reaction, and you think it's food-related (which is usually when it will manifest in poop trouble), speak to your veterinarian about trying an elimination diet. They should be able to recommend a hypoallergenic meal plan that can help you eliminate all common allergens. Then you can try to add them back in one at a time to see what is causing the problem.

Food allergies often result in intestinal distress and symptoms like excess gas and very loose stools. In those cases, your dog might not be able to make it outside to do their business. Help them by finding the root cause of the problem and taking it out of their diet.

Hiring Help

Whether you can't be home during the day with your puppy or you're looking for a long-term option to take your dog out once or twice a day, sometimes, you have to look for outside help.

Hiring someone to help with your dogs is a lot like hiring a childminder, though. You wouldn't trust just anyone to take care of them, and you shouldn't when you hire a dog sitter or walker. Here are a few things you should consider and ask when you are looking for a helper:

- Ask about their experience working with dogs. You do not want to hire someone who has never worked with dogs before. They don't exactly have to be a veterinarian, but someone with experience working in a boarding kennel, grooming parlor, or dog trainer will have the right kind of skills.

- Ask for references. A good pet sitter will be able to give you references to people they have worked for before.
- Ask about their schedule. If they are very busy or have other commitments like university or school, they might not be able to be there when you need them. Do you have a backup plan? A formal service might be a better fit if not.
- Ask them to come to your home and meet your dogs. You will have to introduce them to your pups anyway. Watch how they interact and react.

Once you have chosen someone to take care of your dog's daily walks, make sure that they know which kind of leash they prefer and what their schedule is. You want to stick to a routine as closely as possible so that your dog knows when to expect their time outside.

Never be afraid to have a "nanny cam" set up if you will have someone come into your home and interact with your dogs. Even the nicest people can sometimes be different when they are alone, and you are trusting them with members of your family.

Post Kennel Problems

In most cases, if you put your dog in a boarding kennel, you don't have too much to worry about. However, if they are younger (or more prone to picking up bad habits), the experience of being in a kennel can sometimes make them forget their training.

Boarding kennels often have easy to clean concrete surfaces, which means that instead of going on grass, dirt, or a pee pad like they are used to, your dog might be doing their business on concrete.

If you are only away for a few days, that might not stick. But if you take a longer trip and they are there for a few weeks, they might be "retrained" to go on a different surface. Since it is acceptable at the kennel, they might try to do it when they get home too.

Try to choose a kennel that takes dogs out onto grassed areas daily or uses a more "home-like" surface in their kennel spaces, like stone chips or similar. Anything that doesn't look too much like a surface in your home is better!

When you bring your dog home from the kennel, pay extra attention to their schedule, and make sure you take them out for frequent walks, so they get used to going where you want them to.

To be safe, when you have to leave home for more than a few minutes, consider using a crate to keep your dog in a contained space. But remember that even healthy adult dogs can't hold it for more than about eight hours at a time. Make sure they go before you put them in the crate and as soon as you get back too.

Co-Sleeping Problems

When you bring a new puppy home, they will be away from their mother, siblings, and everything they have ever known. They are also going to be the cutest little ball of fluff you have ever seen!

So, when they are awake at 2am, singing the song of their people because they're lonely and sad, it's tempting to bring them into your bed and let them snuggle.

This is a very bad idea, for several reasons.

Firstly, puppies are tiny, and you can easily hurt them as you move around in your sleep. Younger puppies especially will not be able to move out of the way as you move, which can be very dangerous.

But, as we have already mentioned, young puppies need to pee about every half hour (or sometimes even more frequently.) If you thought listening to them crying was terrible for your sleep, just wait until you wake up in a warm puddle of puppy pee!

Give your new puppy a warm blanket and a small toy that they can snuggle up to. Make them a comfy and safe area to sleep in, with an easily accessible place to do their business. And wait to potentially bring them into your bed until they're bigger and have better bladder control!

Outdoor Safety

When they are older, most dogs can be trusted in the backyard on their own for a little while, at least. You might find that you have a digger or a chewer, but those are problems for another book.

However, when puppies are very young, they are not able to be outside by themselves. Even the safest-looking backyard is full of all sorts of potential puppy pitfalls.

Fishponds and swimming pools that aren't securely fenced are drowning hazards.

Tiny puppies could be targeted by predators or even large predatory birds.

There may be hazardous items that could fall on them without warning or sharp objects that might hurt them.

People have even been known to steal puppies from fenced yards.

You should never leave a young puppy alone outside for any amount of time. If you can't take your puppy out and supervise them while they do their business, place them in their indoor pee pad area.

If you need to go inside while they are outside, pick them up, take them with you, and place them in their puppy area.

All it takes is a few moments for something dangerous or tragic to happen, and it is just not worth the risk. Treat your puppy the way you would a human baby. You can't leave either of them alone in areas that are not purposely made for safety for any amount of time.

Let Old Dogs Teach New Dogs Tricks

If you already have dogs, you might find it a lot easier to train your new puppy to go where they all go.

It all goes back to the concept of dogs being pack animals. Older dogs will already know the rules, and puppies will want to make friends with them, so they're likely to follow them around like, well, puppy dogs!

You want to be careful when introducing new puppies to your older dogs, and of course, you can't leave them alone together while your puppy is tiny. But they will almost certainly try to imitate their older "brothers and sisters."

Make sure you supervise all their time together, especially when your pup is very young, and correct any aggressive behavior as soon as you see it.

Create a "Go-To" Spot

Training your new puppy or dog to go where you want them to is a big deal, and when they do start consistently going outside, it's going to feel like a big victory.

But just going anywhere outside is also not ideal.

Dog urine is not great for grass, so if they choose to use the same spot on your lawn every time they go, you will have bald patches to deal with. Most dogs will also try to "cover" their spot when they go. If they do this when they're in your flower beds, you will have nasty surprises when you're planting petunias and a messy bed!

Male dogs often choose a metal or wooden pole or stake to go on, but over time, the chemicals in urine can cause them to rust or rot.

None of this is ideal, so if you're noticing that your backyard is a bathroom free for all, you need to do a little more training.

Restrict access to areas you don't want your dogs to go with fences or similar barriers. Encourage them to go to a particular area by using dog runs or similar to keep them in a specific spot. Even better if they are portable, so you can move them around to prevent lawn problems.

If you can create an area with pea gravel that your dog can use to do their bathroom thing, you'll have the perfect place for urine to drain away and make clean up that much easier. Rain or a quick hose will wash away all the smells too!

Of course, if you take your dog for walks outside of the house, make sure you always pick up their mess. Dispose of it in an outside garbage can or flush it down the toilet to avoid smells and confusion.

More Potty Tips

There's a lot of information in this book, and none of it is one size fits all. You're going to have to adapt some of the ideas to suit your family, your home, and your dog. Some of the basics will always apply, like cleanup and not using punishment as a tool, but you will find that you need to try things out to see what works.

While you do that, there are several more potty tips that can make your life a little easier:

- Avoid long car trips until your puppy is at least mostly potty trained. If they can't hold it for half an hour in your home, they can't hold it in your car, and cars are usually harder to clean!

- If you have a dog or puppy that is a poop eater, be sure to clean up all poop from all your pets as soon as you can. Many dogs aren't too picky about whose poop they eat!

- As a general rule of thumb for very young puppies, if they've just eaten, they're going to need to go soon. Don't wait!

- Invest in a gentle, frequent use shampoo. When you're dealing with very young puppies, you can expect pretty frequent, messy situations. You don't want to dry their skin out with harsh chemicals.

- Get a sizeable outdoor garbage can with a lid if you don't already have one. Pee pads and other training aids will start piling up soon, and if you try to use your indoor garbage cans to get rid of them, you're going to have a very stinky house!

- You shouldn't have your puppy too much before they are about 12 weeks old, but if you do, understand that very young puppies won't be able to start potty training until they reach at least that age and some aren't ready until about 16 weeks.

- Puppies usually also need to go after they wake

up. So, make sure you take them outside or to their toilet area as soon as they wake up.

- As your puppy gets older, look for signs like barking, sniffing, scratching at doors, and similar as signs they want to go out. Encourage this behavior, so they will keep asking to go out.

- If you use a crate for your puppy, make sure it's the right size and that they don't stay in it for too long. Even an older puppy should never spend more than three or four hours in a crate – and if they do, they should be able to access water.

- If you make significant changes (like moving to a new house or putting in a new carpet) while your puppy is potty training, you might find that they get confused and have more accidents. Stick to your schedule to get them back on track.

- Even when your puppy is older and mostly trained, be sure to check hidden corners from time to time. Sometimes, rather than ask to go out, they will find a quiet, unseen corner to do their business.

Potty training a puppy or a dog can feel like taking one step forward and two steps back sometimes, but consistency is key. Keep reinforcing the behavior you want and stick to a schedule that works for you and your dog. Eventually, they will get the hang of it, and the accidents will be a thing of the past.

TO ERR IS HUMAN — TO FORGIVE, CANINE.

- Unknown

Afterword

Having a dog is a huge responsibility. They rely on you for everything from their food and water to training them and teaching them how to behave the way you would like them to.

Dogs don't instinctively know that you don't want them to go to the bathroom on the rug, so you have to show them. But they definitely do live to please their owners, so you will get where you want to go with the right strategy and positive reinforcement.

Some of the issues you will face when you are potty training a puppy or dog are natural, like the amount their bladder can hold and for how long. But some can be controlled, like the type of food you feed and the strategies you use to teach them the behaviors you want.

The training process can take anything from four months to as much as a year, but it will get easier as you go along.

If you find that your older dog or puppy is having many accidents, it might not be because your training is not working. Consider external factors, like medical conditions or the type of food you are feeding them, and make sure that you reassure your dog when there are significant changes in your life.

If you have read this book and you don't think you have the time or energy to devote to many months of potty training, or that you can commit to setting and sticking to a schedule that will help your dog develop good toilet habits, it might not be the right time to get a dog.

If you live in a small apartment, and you can't imagine taking a large dog for walks several times a day, you might need to consider getting a smaller dog who can use an indoor or balcony-based toilet area.

You can set your puppy or dog up for success in potty training by considering your living situation, the time you have available, and how you plan to approach the process. You can also set them up to fail, which will leave both of you unhappy.

You will need to teach your dog many other things, from socializing with other animals and people to obedience training. But the very first, fundamental thing that will set you up for success is to teach them good toilet habits.

Hopefully, with this information, you can do just that. In which case, welcome to the dog owner family, and to many years of beautiful, unconditional puppy love!

THERE IS NO PSYCHIATRIST IN THE WORLD LIKE A PUPPY LICKING YOUR FACE.

- Ben Williams

Thank You

Thank you for reading this book and allowing us to share our knowledge with you.

If you've enjoyed this book, please let us know by leaving an Amazon rating and a brief review! It only takes about 30 seconds, and it helps us compete against big publishing houses. It also helps other readers find our work!

Thank you for your time, and have an awesome day!

Made in the USA
Monee, IL
29 July 2023

40129041R00075